My Shadow

Shadow Work for Beginners

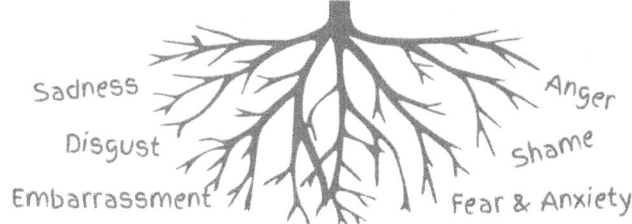

A GUIDED JOURNAL / WORKBOOK

The information contained in this book is for general information purposes only and should not be considered a substitute for the advice of a mental health professional.

By Avery Munjhani
Copyright © 2022 all rights reserved
JH Publications

Bonus Freebie!

Looking for more Journaling Prompts?
Get my Quick Start Shadow Work Guide!
'14 Day Shadow Work Journaling Challange' for FREE!
Simply go to:
https://bit.ly/14DaySW
or scan the QR Code below

Sharing is Caring

I want to truly thank you for giving Shadow Work a try. It has saved my life, and I hope it can the same for you and others.

Because this work has done so much for me, I am giving away **free, printable PDF** files of this book for anyone who purchased it.
Not only so that you can use this journal more than once, but also so you have the ability to share it with whoever may need it.

If you would like one, please just send me an email with your request to:
averymunjhani@jhpublications.com

Furthermore I want to invite you to reach out at any point should you have questions, or simply want to share your story.

I am committed to reading and responding to every inquiry personally.

If you've received this journal as a gift, the person that gave it to you truly cares about you.

If you decided to acquire this journal yourself, great, thats a sign of self-love!

If you found this journal because I lost it, please return to:

Welcome!

Here is a quick overview of what you can expect

- A commitment contract to help you stay on track and remind you of your goals

- A short introduction on how to do Shadow Work and use this journal

- 90 journaling prompts to guide you through your journey, uncover and transcend your shadows.

- Plenty of free space to record your thoughts, feelings and revelations

- Bonus Entry: A letter to your future self

Before we begin..

In order for you to make the most out of this shadow work journal, I would like you to accept and sign the following commitment contract with yourself:

As of today, I, _Tyran McNown_, will take the courage to commit to the journey of self-healing and self-discovery.

I promise to start and finish this commitment by being truthful with every word I write in this journal. I will express myself freely on every page and take my time working on each prompt.

I am aware of all the hardships this process can cause me, but I will learn to accept and be patient with myself.

It may not be possible for me to heal my shadows at once, but I can use them to improve my well-being.

As I collect every piece of myself, I will continue to persevere and heal every part that has been broken.

I believe that this journey is not just for my own good, but will also positively impact other people around me.

I am looking forward to knowing myself better.

_7·9·2023_
STARTING DATE

Tyran McNown
SIGNATURE

EVERYONE CARRIES A SHADOW, AND THE LESS IT IS EMBODIED IN THE INDIVIDUAL'S CONSCIOUS LIFE, THE BLACKER AND DENSER IT IS.

- Carl Jung

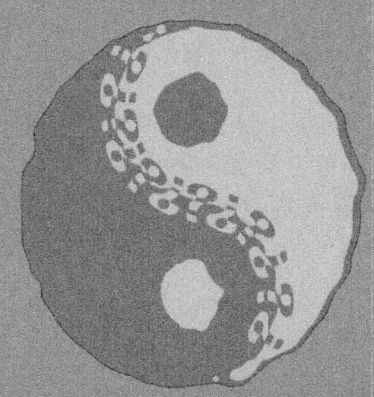

Introduction

We all have shadows. They can be found underneath the mask we wear every day. They are the things we do not want other people to see. We keep them all inside and go on with life as if these shadows do not exist.

But how long can you conceal them? How long can you convince yourself you are okay? How long can you keep these shadows that are blocking your way to achieving healing and self-growth?

There will come a time when you need to face these shadows and change into a better version of yourself.

And that time is now.

In this journal, you will have an opportunity to reflect on your shadows. The part you choose to keep to yourself and from the people around you. You will learn to accept the good and the bad side of your personality and work with them to improve yourself.

But before you dive in, you first need to understand what this activity is all about and how it will benefit you in the long run.

With all that said, let me introduce you to the concept of the 'Shadow-Self' and 'Shadow Work'.

What is the 'shadow'?

With his other concepts, including Anima, Persona, and Self, the Shadow is one of the archetypes coined by Swiss psychologist Carl Jung. According to Jung, Shadow is based on the idea that every human has self-sabotaging behaviors or the darker side of the personality we consider undesirable. Hence, we reject it as part of ourselves.

Often, the shadow self is a defense mechanism or projection we show to other people. We revert to it because the negative emotion is too overwhelming for us to control.

For example, you often judge other people on how they look, because deep down, you are unaware of your own insecurities. You fear someone will do the same to you, so you point it out in others instead.

Your shadow self can also be affected by the environment you live in or the people you associate yourself with throughout your life.

Traumatic experiences from the past may also cause you to become more sensitive to your feelings or how you interact with other people. Because of these scenarios, you start to build shadow traits such as anger, jealousy, manipulation, selfishness, arrogance, obsessiveness, judgment, and stubbornness.

This kind of behavior remains deeply rooted within us. If you continue to suppress it inside, you will become unsatisfied with your life and miss the opportunity to change yourself for the better.

The best method to address these issues is by doing Shadow Work.

What is Shadow Work?

Shadow Work is the process of learning about your shadow self on the journey to self-growth and improvement. The Shadow work journal serves as a guide for precisely that. It will help you to practice mindfulness, reflect, and learn how to deal with your shadows effectively.

When we do 'Shadow Work', we shine a light on these dark parts of our being. And while this can be a very difficult and painful practice, exposing and accepting them will lead to enormous personal growth.

Doing shadow work allows us to deal with and overcome past trauma. It can help you realize the source of your negative beliefs and your worst habits. Surface memories you had long forgotten or have been suppressing, and confront them.

Shadow work gives us an opportunity at self-healing, reflection, and self-discovery. This journal provides you with 90 prompts to guide you through your journey. Some prompts you will find easier to answer than others. Answering these prompts will help you surface deeply repressed feelings and traumas. Try to acknowledge those emotions and personality traits about yourself. Welcome and thank them. You will notice an unexpected feeling of peace in many areas of your life.

And while your ego might be telling you right now that there's nothing you are hiding or repressing, I assure you there always is. Think back to when you were a child. Did your parents ever tell you that you shouldn't feel a certain way? Feelings you weren't allowed to express? These emotions will feed your shadow.

Or think about the last time you judged someone for something they had done. Or felt offended by someone's actions or words. In most cases, what annoys us most about others are the traits we inherit ourselves. But we repress these traits and try to ignore them. Oftentimes by simply revealing and accepting them, we are able to let go of any anger or judgement.

Shadow work isn't often joyful, but it's always cathartic.

There will be some days where you will dread doing the work, and on those days it's usually most important that we do it. It is desirable to stay as consistent as you can with your daily practice.

Why you need to do the work

Working on your shadow will help you work through and overcome past traumas. Our emotions are not something that should rule us. We should aim to live a more balanced life. Only by accepting our emotions as they arise, are we able to let them go. We don't need to react to our anger or hurt the way we are used to.

Free yourself from your shadow ruling your emotions from the darkness.

The goal is to learn self-acceptance. To learn to love yourself again, and to deal with your negative emotions in a healthy, constructive way. By learning about and understanding our triggers, we are able to become more self aware of our feelings, as they arise. Soon you will feel like you are in more control, and have more power over yourself and your emotions.

Shadow work is a tool for self-discovery. It will help you work towards your dream. By identifying your excuses, you can think about what it would be like to approach your problems and obstacles in life without them.

Your shadow will always be with you, and you should be thankful for it. It is not there to hurt. In fact it's there to protect you from re-living traumas from your past. You can work with your shadow, shine a light and help release these negative emotions.

When working with these prompts, always approach yourself with kindness and an open heart. And by the end of each day you will feel like a happier and healthier human being.

How to do Shadow Work

When you are looking for hidden objects buried deep within, the only way to find them is by digging. But first, you need to gather all the necessary tools to bring with you. These may include a shovel, a trowel, or even a pickaxe if you need to break some boulders. You might also need a map to know where you have to start and a lamp to illuminate your path.

Once you unearth an item that's been buried for a long time, you can see a lot of dust and dirt around it. Even if you can already see and hold the actual item in your hand, you may still not recognize what it actually is unless you remove the grimes.

The process is similar when you uncover your dark side, or what we are referring to as the Shadow.

The purpose of doing Shadow Work is to help you dig through the deepest part of your soul, memories, and emotions and to shine a light on them. And it is not enough for you to just recognize your negative traits. You need to know the origin and the factors that trigger those emotions in the first place.

By doing shadow work, you will have a chance to surface all these hidden traits and resolve each of your issues, one at a time. This process might bring up some unpleasant emotions. You might feel depressed, hurt, fearful, shameful, numb, guilty, and abandoned at some point, but it is all part of the process. And a common manifestation of doing shadow work, is that you start to become more mindful and aware of the traits you have repressed for so long.

The most effective solution to know oneself is by practicing mindfulness.

How To Use This Journal

A last few tips before you begin.

#1 Always be kind to yourself.
You've made choices in your life, and you can't go back and change them. Unpleasant or unwanted feelings and thoughts may surface. It's important to understand that these are what made you who you are today. So be kind to yourself as you heal those memories and traumas.

#2 Consider your shadow work a ceremony, and practice it as such
Set aside some time for your shadow work every day. (30-60 minutes). Make yourself a special, cozy place, where you feel comfortable to do the work. Light some candles and/or incense, get a glass of your favorite beverage, put on some music, or anything else that will help you feel relaxed and at peace. You could even get yourself a special pen.
Treat this like a personal, sacred daily ritual.

#3 Take deep breaths and calm your mind before you start writing
I recommend spending 5-10 minutes before each ceremony on a simple meditation. Start taking very slow, deep breaths. If it helps you can count along in your head, 5 seconds in, 5 seconds out. Acknowledge any thought or emotions that arise, and simply let them pass. When you catch yourself caught in a train of thought, just return to your breath. You will notice that whatever burdened you today keeps coming to your mind. It's Okay. Accept what happened, let it go, and return to your breath.

#4 Don't start writing right away
I know, this sounds a little silly because you probably really want to get started. But here is what I mean: When reading the daily prompt, let it sit for a minute or two. Try to notice what comes up when you read the words. Reread the prompt if you happen to get lost in a particular thought. Then take one more deep breath before you start writing.

#5 Be as consistent as possible
Being realistic, there will be some days where we aren't able to find the time, energy, or motivation to do the work. And that is okay! Again, be kind to yourself. You can always start again the next day. But I want to emphasize that daily practice will lead to the best results. If you happen to miss a day, take some time instead to think about what the reason for that was. What triggered or influenced your decision? What feelings did you experience when you made the decision?

Most of the shadows of this life are caused by standing in one's own sunshine.

-Ralph Waldo Emerson

Lets Begin!

DAY 1: Childhood Dreams

Do you still remember the very first dream you had when you were young? It can be what you answered when your parents or teachers asked you what you want to be when you grow up.
List that/those dream/s here. What do you think you had those dreams in the first place? Do you still have those dreams? Or have they changed now that you are older?

When I was 4, I wanted to be a neurosurgeon. I did a presentation on split-brain surgery on career day in Kindergarten. Then that moved to a PA, and then ER Nurse.

I think I had these dreams.
1. My knowing I am here to help people
2. My Moms' influence
3. Knowing both of my parents were in the Medical field

I still want to help & heal others. My ideal 'dream job' would be a Medicine Woman of some sort.

DAY 2 : Worst Traits

We all have undesirable traits that we may consciously or unconsciously act out during our daily life. Try to remember some recent interactions; what are the worst things you have witnessed in other people? Do you believe some of the traits you see in other people are also embodied by yourself sometimes?

I see a lot of entitlement and selfishness. Mainly just snobby, snooty people.

Then mainly those that seem so preoccupied with everything & everyone else that I wonder why I'm even part of their life.

I think I embody or have embodied most of these at least once in my life

DAY 3: Reflections

Just like a mirror, we unconsciously use other people to perceive a reflection of ourselves. When you look someone else in the eye, what do you think is the kind of reflection they will show you? How do you think they would describe you? What would you feel after seeing the image of yourself in their eyes?

It depends on the nature of the relationship between me & them.

People that don't know me would probably think I'm a bitch because I try not to interact w/ anyone.

Otherwise maybe a decent-looking lady, albeit a little chubby ~ but cool tattoos

My tribe would see my awkward, but kinda funny mom/ artist/healer

No matter what - I'd feel awkward.

DAY 4: Irrational Feelings

There are days when you do not feel very joyful. What do you think are the factors that can trigger you to unleash a negative emotion and ruin your day? What do you think these irrational feelings are rooted in? Can you recall a situation when you unexpectedly burst out all of your emotions and tended to do something you regret later on?

Feeling inadequate, like I didn't measure up. Or if things just keep not going as planned. Also - when I feel like I've disappointed someone that I care about.

I feel like some of it stems from my mom doing everything possible in order to "keep up appearances"

I had one of those yesterday

It happens a lot.

DAY 5: The worst of worst traits

It is normal to feel your worst at times. There will be days when you cannot avoid feeling sad or disappointed. You might feel like you have been abandoned, forgotten, or betrayed. But among these worst traits, what is the one you consider the worst among them based on your encounters?

The worst trait for me to feel is like I don't matter

DAY 6: Disappointments

When was the last time you felt disappointed in yourself? Narrate your experience below. Explain the reason why you think you felt that way. What do you think is the factor that triggers you to feel down?

Yesterday~

Felt super overwhelmed because I feel like I can't keep up with everything and I can't accomplish what I typically am able because of my surgical recovery. That made me feel like I'm not valuable to Kenny and he'll just replace me. Because I don't matter.

DAY 7: Relationship Boundaries

No man is an island. Every one of us in this world needs connections and relationships to help us grow. How's your relationship with the people around you —family, friends, colleagues, partner, etc.? Do you have any boundaries set on each of them? What made you decide on these boundaries?

DAY 8: Emtpy Feelings

Sometimes we feel empty inside. Without any clear direction or goal. During these times, what do you do to make yourself feel better? Or to find your way back to your true path?

I smudge, I give myself readings. I go into nature. I listen to music & sing my ass off. I make art, clean, or go to my local thrift store.

DAY 9: Influences

We all have someone we look up to and aspire to be. It can be a family member, a close friend, a mentor, or even a celebrity. Which among these people do you think influences you the most in almost every aspect of your life? Explain why and tell a story on when you realized you like this person the most.

DAY 10: Envy and Jealousy

Envy and jealousy occur when you feel discontented. You often compare yourself to other people. You think they are doing better than you. Do you feel envious and/or jealous of someone? What do you think is/are the reason/s? Is it good or bad? How can you work these feelings out?

Mostly I only tend to feel that way when I observe a relationship that I want or when it comes to looks. Or if I feel like someone doesn't deserve what they have.

It's ALL FUCKING STUPID!

Um... kinda why I got this book.

DAY 11: Being Misunderstood

Children often get misunderstood. Do you remember any situation when you were a child and you felt you were wronged? How did you react? Can you tell if it affected you as you were growing up?

When I was bullied in elementary school. I was misunderstood and judged.

It still affects me now. And I hate that it does

DAY 12 : Burning Bridges & Building Walls

Not all people you meet will stay with you. There will come a time when you have to walk away from a certain relationship. Maybe it is too toxic or is it holding you back from being the kind of person you want to be.
Can you still remember that person who you walked away from? What was the reason you cut your ties with that person? Has anything changed in your life since then?

I walked away from my ex Patrick. I was just tired of being treated like I was unworthy and being mistreated and cheated on.

My life has been kind of a shit show. But I have a 0 tolerance policy for cheating.

DAY 13: Shameful Memories

We all have memories we try to forget because they bring us shame. What are memories you have that still haunt you today?

- Getting caught w/ alcohol @ a H.S. football game.
- When my mom found out I had sex
- A few boyfriends
- Being cheated on by ex-hus & exbff
- Getting arrested
- Getting felonies
- Getting addicted to meth
- Making

DAY 14: Reminiscing Shameful Memories

But what if you can go back in time and relive this shameful memory again. Close your eyes and recall every detail of that memory. Will you choose to change it? What do you think you can learn from it?

DAY 15: Parents and Caregivers

Your experiences and outlook in life were greatly influenced by the people who took care of you when you were young. It can be your parents, grandparents, aunts, uncles, teachers, etc.
List all the people you can remember who helped and guided you growing up. Then, write the positive and negative traits they have based on your interactions with them. Which of their characteristics has manifested in you?

DAY 16: Who controls your emotions?

Among the people that surround you, who do you think is the one who influences you the most, the one who often belittles you, or the one who always brings you down? Do you think that person has more control over your emotions than yourself?

DAY 17: Unhealthy Relationships

Have you had any unhealthy relationships before? Do you see a common pattern among these relationships which made them unhealthy for you? What do you think you can do to avoid such relationships in the future?

DAY 18: The Worst in You

Have you experienced a situation that brought out the absolute worst in you? What do you think that was? What exactly happened that led you to unleash that kind of emotion?

DAY 19: Self-Sabotage

Can you still remember the first time you ever self-sabotaged or did something destructive in your life? What did you exactly feel during that time? What do you think was the factor that triggered you?

DAY 20: Broken Trust

You build relationships with the people around you by establishing a solid foundation made of trust.
Every person we love, we trust. But what if this person you cherish the most breaks your heart and betrays you? How would you react?
Have you had an experience like this before? If yes, what will you tell the person who hurt you and broke your trust? If not, what are ways in which you fear someone might break your trust in the future?

DAY 21: A Letter to the Person who hurt you most

You may still be avoiding this moment when you need to remember the one who hurt you the most. If you still feel uncomfortable, it is an indication that you have not forgiven this person yet, and you are still keeping this negative feeling inside.

You cannot always run away. You may not necessarily face the person who hurt you again, but you can face the fact that you can heal your wound from the pain that this person caused you.

Take this moment to write that person a letter. Write every unsaid word. Pour out all your emotions. This is your chance to say everything you want to say, so you can prepare yourself to forgive.

DAY 22: Greater Than or Less Than

When do you think you felt inferior or better than the person you were envious or jealous about? Has it crossed your mind that you may be on an equal footing with that person in some aspect?

DAY 23: Failure

What is the thing you consider the biggest failure in your life? Why do you think it is a failure? Share your story below.

DAY 24: People who Inspire You

You may have someone you look up to in your life. And this person inspires you to be your best in everything you do. But have you ever contemplated what exactly you like so much about this person? What do you think they have that you also want to possess? Describe that person and the traits that make you look up to them.

DAY 25: Overthinking

Overthinking is an indication of an underlying mental health disorder. Were there any instances when you found yourself overthinking about what happened in the past, unable to stop replaying the memory in your head? What were you going through at that time?

DAY 26: Values and Passion

Can you measure the importance of your core values? Can you say that these values and beliefs influenced what you are currently passionate about?

DAY 27: Good Enough

Because of self-doubt, you may feel that you are not good enough at things you are doing in your life. But in reality, it is a lie. What do you think might be the reason you feel you are not good enough?

DAY 28: Self-Opinion

How do you perceive yourself as a human? Do you think you have a better understanding of yourself?

DAY 29: Forgiving

There may be mistakes you've made in the past that you have not forgiven yourself for. It is now time for you to embrace forgiveness. You can never move on with life if things still hold you back.
Address that situation by writing it below. Pour out your emotions and express forgiveness toward yourself.

DAY 30: Emotional Attachments

Are there any unhealthy emotional attachments you formed easily in the past? Do you think there is a tendency to form unhealthy attachments and make it hard for you to create a healthy and meaningful relationship? Why do you think this happens?

THE PERSON YOU CALL AN ENEMY IS AN EXAGGERATED ASPECT OF YOUR OWN SHADOW SELF.

- Deepak Chopra

Well done, you've completed the first 30 Days!

It's time for a little check-in.

How are you feeling so far? Have you had days that were overwhelming? Did you already uncover parts of yourself that you were never aware of?

Take a little bit of time to reflect on the last 30 days.

And most importantly, give yourself a pad on the back!

You are committed to this, and your future self will surely thank you for it.

DAY 31: Core Values

Did your parents or guardians establish specific core values you had to follow while growing up? List them all down. Do you still hold these values now, or have they changed?

DAY 32 : Pastime and Hobbies

There are days when you have nothing else to do. During times when you are bored, what do you usually do? Are there any activities you enjoy doing or want to do more often? What brings you joy on a boredom-filled day, and why?

DAY 33: Negative Emotions

What is a negative emotion you do not want to feel anymore? What do you think is the reason behind this?

DAY 34: A Letter to the Person you find hard to forgive

Take this chance to think of the person you struggled to forgive. Write a letter to express your feelings toward that person.
Please do your best to find ways to forgive this person for what they have done.

DAY 35: The Weight of Traumas

Can you remember a traumatic experience from your childhood? How did it affect your life? What action do you think you take to work through this trauma and move past it?

DAY 36: Processing Emotions

How do you usually process your emotions? How about negative emotions? Have you noticed any changes over time? What are those changes?

DAY 37: The Biggest Lie You ever Told Yourself

Most humans lie. Sometimes the intentions behind a lie are egotistical. But I believe more often we lie to protect someone. We do not want to hurt their feelings or our own.

Have you ever told a lie to yourself? What was the biggest lie you ever told yourself?

DAY 38: Fear of Darkness

When you were a child, were you afraid of the dark? Explain a scenario where you felt scared and why.

Examine yourself and try to find the root of your fear of darkness.

DAY 39: Mirror Work

Your reflection is one of the most effective ways to see your hidden shadow self.

Get a mirror. Stare at yourself for a while. Make sure you look directly into your eyes. What are the thoughts that come into your mind first upon seeing your reflection? Do you feel uncomfortable or awkward? Do you feel more aware of yourself?

DAY 40: Support System

This is a space where you will have an opportunity to write about anyone or anything you feel that can support you whenever you are struggling with yourself. Take this moment to remember every single one of them. Try to think of a way to express your gratitude toward them.

DAY 41: Distractions

What is/are the things/things that distract you the most? What can you do to stop them from distracting you and disturbing your peace?

DAY 42: Apology

Who do you think is the person/are the people who owe you an apology? And why?

DAY 43: Regret

What is your biggest regret in life? Share a story about a time when you felt extremely regretful.

DAY 44: Self-Improvement

Do you often compare yourself to other people? What do you think is the reason? Do you want to be like that person? There is nothing wrong with comparing yourself to other people since it can better yourself in some aspects.

In what areas do you want to see yourself improve? List them all down and make a plan on what you can do to help yourself improve.

DAY 45: Family Relationships

Is the depth of your relationship with your family different from when you were young and when you grew up? What was it like when you were still a child? Did you often bond with your parents and siblings back then? Did something change as you age? Share your story about your family here.

DAY 46: Worst Childhood Memory

As children, we all did some shameful things that we now feel a lot of regret for. Based on your experiences, which is the worst childhood memory you do not want to remember or other people to know?

DAY 47: If Only...

If only you could change an outcome of a particular situation in your life, what would that be, and what would you do to change it?

DAY 48: Are you too Hard on Yourself?

In what situation do you become too hard on yourself? Where do you think this feeling is rooted? Can you promise to start being more kind to yourself instead? You can write a personal vow to remind you to be more gentle and kinder to yourself when situations get too hard or aren't going your way.

DAY 49: Strengths and Weaknesses

What do you think are your strengths and weaknesses? List them all here.

DAY 50: Love Yourself More

Now that you have reached this point in your journey to self-healing and self-discovery, can you say you love yourself more? Or is there still something that keeps you from accepting the reality of how lovable and valuable you are?

DAY 51: Misconceptions

There's a saying that first impressions last. When you first meet a person, you will tend to judge this person's personality at a glance. But as you get to know that person, you realize they are not what you think they were.

Now that you are meeting your shadow self, do you happen to think of any misconceptions about your own being? List them all here and explain why you mistook yourself for that kind of personality.

DAY 52: Ideal Self

Halfway through this journal, you have already met a lot of your shadow parts. As you encounter them, you might realize that some might not be so bad compared to others. Among these negative traits, which one keeps you from taking one step closer to your ideal self?

DAY 53: Memory Deletion

There are many memories you want to keep and cherish. But there are also things that you want to erase from your memory. What is a memory that you want to delete forever, and why? What would the impact on your life be if you erased this memory as if it never existed in the first place? If there are multiple memories, feel free to write about each of those.

DAY 54: An Image of Your Shadow Self

If you could draw an image of your shadow self, what would you imagine it to look like? What kind of beliefs, emotions, thoughts, and traits do you think it would have?

DAY 55: Setting Up Boundaries

Setting up boundaries with people around you is like establishing guidelines on how you want them to treat you. Do you personally set up boundaries among your circle? How do you feel when people neglect the boundaries you have established towards them? Do you feel disrespected, offended, etc.?

DAY 56: Addictions

Is there any kind of addiction present in your life now? Where do you think you got this addition from? Who may have influenced you that lead you to have this kind of addiction? Can you develop an action plan to overcome it?

DAY 57. You Against the World

Are there any situations when you feel like it is just you against the world? Why do you think is you feel so alone and like you have to face all these struggles on your own?

DAY 58: Facing Judgements

Do you often receive judgments from other people, especially those close to you? What do you feel about their opinions of you? Do you experience being judged more frequently?

DAY 59: Biggest Fears

What do you think are the three things you fear the most? Why do you fear them? Try to dig deep. Many of our fears stem from a traumatic childhood experience.

DAY 60: Safe Place

With everything that's currently happening in the world, do you feel like you are living in a safe place? When you feel afraid, lost, or alone, where do you seek refuge for comfort and to make you feel safe?

EVERY PAIN, ADDICTION, ANGUISH, LONGING, DEPRESSION, ANGER OR FEAR IS AN ORPHANED PART OF US SEEKING JOY, SOME DISOWNED SHADOW WANTING TO RETURN TO THE LIGHT AND HOME OF OURSELVES.

- Jacob Nordby

Congratulations for getting this far!

You can be proud of yourself!

I know very few people who actually follow through on their commitments regarding self-growth and personal development.

How about treating yourself today? After all, you are deserving of your own love.

Before you start the last stretch of this journal, I want you to reflect on the last 60 days.

What has changed since the start of this workbook? Do you get the feeling you know yourself better?

DAY 61: Solving Conflicts

When you have a conflict with someone, what is your initial reaction? Do you tend to avoid that person right away and wait for them to initiate the first move or go after them and try to resolve the matter?

DAY 62: Expectations and Disappointments

You think you know the people that are closest to you well. And that you can trust them. But every once in a while, be it intentionally or not, you get let down by someone.

When was the last time someone let you down in a way that you didn't expect them to?

Why did you feel let down? Do you think you reacted rationally or did you let your emotions take over?

DAY 63: Unconditional Love

Do you think you can love other people without any conditions? If yes, do you believe there might be someone out there who could do the same for you?

DAY 64: Suppressed Feelings

What do you think is an emotion you usually choose to suppress? Take this moment to recall any situation from your past where you choose to repress your feelings.

Write down the situation, and try to connect with that emotion. Then, practice feeling it, process it, breathe it out, and let it go.

DAY 65: Major Complaints

What are things that make you complain about other people? Why do you think you feel so negative towards them? What do you think triggers you to complain about what others do, feel, or think?

DAY 66: Self-Care

Is doing self-care your priority? If not, what do you think you can do to further encourage yourself into taking care of your well-being? What practices should you be doing now to start being more mindful of yourself?

DAY 67: Unanswered Questions

What was a question you often asked yourself when you were growing up, and you still don't know the solution to? Take this moment to think of it and seek the answer yourself.

DAY 68: Spoil Yourself

What is your favorite way to self-soothe or rejuvenate yourself? In your mind, what would the perfect self-care day look like? List all your ideas here and explore how you can do each of them.

DAY 69: Wearing a Different Mask

In what situation do you find yourself wearing a different mask or persona? What do you think would happen if you exposed your true self?

DAY 70: Friendships

Which of your friends make you feel safe, secure, and loved? And which tends to leave you feeling isolated, pressured, or otherwise uncomfortable?

DAY 71: Overcoming Fears

Fears prevent you from moving forward. If there are any fears you still find challenging to overcome, take this opportunity to list them all out. By keeping track of these fears, you will know how you can control your life for the better. Or even find a way to move past some of them.

DAY 72: Self-acceptance

After doing the work for a while, do you think you can say you already accept your shadows? What else can you do to embrace the reality that these shadows will leave scars in you?

Will you choose to conceal or accept them?

DAY 73: No Holding Back

As you face your shadow self, allow it to talk to you about all the negative things it wants to show you. Do not hold back. Just let this emotion flow and try to accept every negative trait your Shadow will throw at you. Be courageous and confront it.

DAY 74: Maturity

Maturity does not come with age. Therefore, do you consider yourself a mature human being? Were there any instances recently where you acted immaturely?

What do you think the people around you would say when asked about your maturity level?

DAY 75: What Drains Your Energy

Can you think of situations that left you feeling drained? Who or what was the reason? What do you think you can address these situations moving forward and avoid feeling drained?

DAY 76: Recurring Negative Thoughts

What is a negative thought that keeps on bothering you? Why do you often think about it?

DAY 77: Insecurities

What do you think are the things that make you feel insecure? Are you insecure with other people?

DAY 78: Overreacting

Do you often overreact about a particular situation? What do you exactly feel when you are getting overboard about something? What do you think are the underlying reasons you tend to feel that way?

DAY 79: Belittled, Demeaned, Ridiculed

When other people look down on you, you might take a hit on your self-esteem and confidence. Have you ever experienced being belittled, demeaned, and ridiculed? What did you feel?

DAY 80: Breaking The Habit

Do you have any habit that is a result of your negative trait? How can you break that habit and overcome it?

DAY 81: Feeling Hurt

Is there someone who hurt you recently? How did they make you feel? Can you remember a time when you were young and had the same feeling? What happened back then? If there is anything, you could say to the person who hurt you, use this space to let it all out.

DAY 82: Observing Your Emotions

Make it a habit to observe your emotions. What are you currently feeling? Take this time to check on your feelings and see if there is anything else you can discover.

DAY 83: Inner Child

Find a picture of yourself when you were still a baby or a child. Look for a place where you can frame and display it. So you can see it more often. Make that picture represent your inner child. Let it remind you that it needs more care from you. Feel free to add some affirmations that will empower you.

DAY 84: Compliments

How do you usually respond to compliments? Do you often express your appreciation or gratitude, or do you often feel awkward?

DAY 85: Disposable Relationships

Which relationships in your life no longer serve you or are becoming toxic? Write about why you feel that way with that person. What exactly happened between you and that person that made you come to this conclusion?

DAY 86: Likes and Dislikes

List out all the things you like and dislike about yourself. For the things you like, what do you think you can do to continue to express them? For the dislikes, what can you do to improve on them?

DAY 87: Nightmares

Do you have recurring nightmares? Do you remember what was happening in your life during that time when you experienced those dreams? Dreams are often the manifestation of your waking life. Your nightmares might be telling you something about your waking life that you are still trying to avoid.

DAY 88: Respect

Do you think other people respect you? Who do you think among your inner circle expresses the most respect to you?

DAY 89: Inner Voice

Whenever you are alone, what do you often tell yourself?

DAY 90: Epiphany

You have made a lot of realizations about yourself and your shadows lately, both the good and the bad. What can you say to yourself right now? Are you happy? Satisfied? Enlightened?

Write everything you want in the space below as you wrap up your shadow work journal.

THE SHADOW IS NEEDED NOW MORE THAN EVER. WE HEAL THE WORLD WHEN WE HEAL OURSELVES, AND HOPE SHINES BRIGHTEST WHEN IT ILLUMINATES THE DARK.

- Sasha Graham

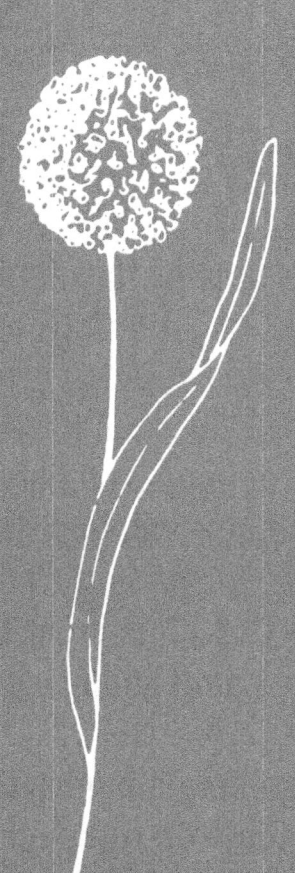

You did it!

Congratulations on reaching this point!

This may be the end of this journal, but it is not the end for you. This is more like a new beginning.

Indeed, the road to self-discovery is a lifelong journey. With this in mind, you need to make sure you bring along all the things you have learned as you go on with your life.

May this shadow work journal help you know yourself better and guide you in overcoming your struggles.

As an optional part, there is one last entry for you to make. One that you can hopefully look back on in a couple of years

an open letter to myself

As your last entry in this journal, I want you to write an open letter to yourself.

In this letter, write about what you have learned during the time of completing this journal.

Which problems and emotions did it helped you deal with?

Think about how you felt everytime after you have completed the work.

And lastly, tell yourself everything thats been on your heart all these years, but you never had the courage to listen.

There is nothing you can't or shouldn't write. After all, this is an open letter.

I've added some extra pages for you, so there is no need to hold back.

In the future you will be able to look at this letter. There always comes a time again where we are in need of doing the shadow work.

Thats when what you are going to tell yourself today will come in very handy.

Before you begin writing, take a few very deep breaths, center yourself, and try to feel the emotion of love.

Try to remember the feeling of loving someone, like a parent or a sibling, and then turn that love towards yourself.

Actively evoke and embrace that love from within for a couple of minutes.

I hope you felt that.. now write!

Dear

> " SHADOW WORK
> IS THE PATH OF
> THE HEART WARRIOR "
>
> *- Carl Jung*

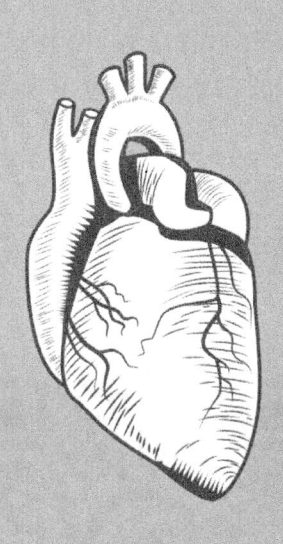

We are here because of you.

We appreciate you, and the time you have commited to completing this workbook. By supporting a small business, you are supporting a dream.

Please leave us an honest review on Amazon.com 🖤

Made in the USA
Coppell, TX
01 July 2023